Flowers Clay
All Seasons Bloom

Copyright © 2020

All rights reserved.

Contents

Red Carnation

This red carnation is ideal for any occasions including wedding, home decoration and hair accessories.

It's a flower of love, passion, affection and adoration.

Tools & materials:

Air dry clay (homemade clay would be nice for flower but you can also buy air dry polymer clay) in green and red color

White PVC glue

Clay knife/ scissor

Rolling pin

Frilling tool

Fork

Floral wire

Preparation time: about 30 minutes

Steps to make red carnation:

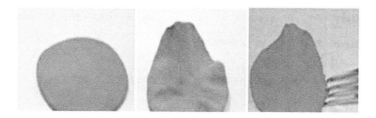

I started my flower by kneading the clay for few minutes until it soft and then make a ball shape with size about 1/2 inch.

After that, I've flatten the ball with rolling pin and frill the edge. No worries if you don't have tool. You can use chopstick though. But don't forget to add a little bit of baby lotion/ oil and frill the edge with this.

The next step is pulling out the edge of the circle with fork.

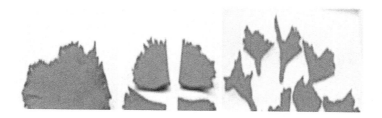

Repeat the above steps and make three pieces of the basic petal.

I cut two of the petals to four pieces each and leave the other one as it is.

I've made 3 slits halfway to the center on the round petal.

Let's go back to the 8 quarter pieces of the petals. Squeeze the tip of the quarter petal and do the same for those 8 quarter pieces of petals.

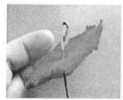

Now, make a small loop at the top of floral wire and then insert it to the center of the petal that was still in one piece .

Close the petal to the center of the loop and at the same time turn the wire clockwise and squeeze the bottom part.

We can then attach all 8 pieces of quarter petals one by one, overlapping each others until you are happy with the flower shape.

Lastly, cover the bottom part of the flower and also the wire with green color clay.

Rose Clay Flower Without Cutter

Alright! Would you prefer rose clay flower in full bloom or bud?

In this tutorial you'll find simple steps to make rosebud without cutter. But if you prefer full bloom rose you can have it by continue adding the petals to the center of the bud.

Material:

Air dry clay like cold porcelain clay (any color as you like). You can make this clay at home with our homemade clay recipe, buy Japanese cold porcelain or soft clay as recommended at what clay to buy page.

PVC glue (Elmer's)

Steps to make rose clay:

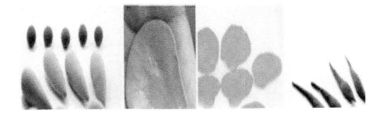

Make seven teardrop shapes. Start by kneading the clay and make a ball shape with diameter about 1-inch. Keep rolling the ball shape and form a teardrop afterward. You might want to check out our clay basic shapes page if you are not sure.

Also roll 3 to 5 smaller ball shapes in green color for calyx and then to teardrop shapes. Pull the sharper edge of the teardrop and flatten this teardrop clay shape on your palm with your index finger. You might have different thickness or length of flatten teardrops. That's okay.

Start making the petals by putting your pink (or other colors) teardrop clay on your palm. Use your thumb to press the clay to form petal shape. Do the same thing for all 7 teardrops.

Take your first petal, roll it from one side to the other side to form the center of the bud. Leave the end of the petal open.

Slip in the second petal from the open side and wrap it around the center.

Get the third petal and wrap it around the second petal. Try to keep the petal's height even.

Continue wrapping the remaining petals. After attaching each petal to the bottom part of flower, pinch the petal form flower base. When you have done wrapping the seven petals, cut the excess clay at the bottom part of flower.

You can now attach the calyx leave. 3 or calyx leave would be sufficient for the bud.

If you prefer open rose, prepare about 13 to 15 petals instead of 7 petals. Attach all petals to the center of the bud by overlapping each petal halfway point of previous one.

You've done with your rose clay flower now. This flower is best for boutonniere, brooch, hair accessories or home decorations.

Calla Lily

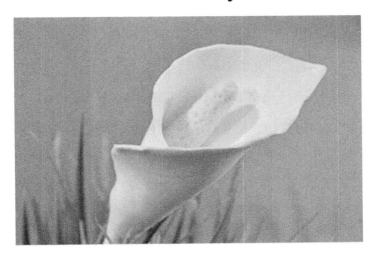

Calla Lily is almost everywhere in Australia but not in Asia. It's kind of rare in the countries like Indonesia, Malaysia and Singapore. It's an expensive flower there.

At certain period of time, this type of Lily flower is favorable for hand bouquet and other wedding decorations.

I like this flower for its simplicity and purity.

And, the best of all is it's very easy to make a bunch of Lily with air dry clay.

Let's have fun....

Materials & Tools

White, yellow and green air dry clay. You might want to check out my homemade clay recipe. If you like to have scented clay, try soapy clay but I would think cold porcelain clay is a better choice for flower making. If you want to buy the clay, Japanese air dry polymer clay is nice for flower.

Rolling pin

Clay knife

Toothpick, needle tool, brush or texture tool

Flower wire

Flower tape (optional)

Baking/ Wax paper

Steps to make Calla Lily:

Roll yellow clay (or other colors) to a tapered sausage shape for stamen at about 5 cm or 2 inches.

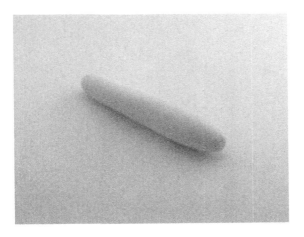

Cut flower wire and wrap it with flower tape or with green color clay. Leave the top part uncovered and insert the wire to the yellow stamen. Use brush or needle to create texture.

Roll white clay color to a ball shape and then change the shape to a teardrop

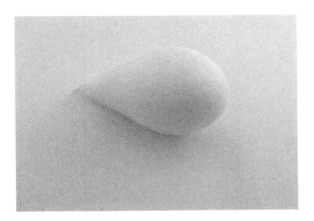

Flatten the teardrop clay shape with your rolling pin. To get a nice petal, cut the clay with your clay knife. Smooth the edges with rolling pin again and lightly pull it out a little bit to make the petal looks natural.

Attach the petal to the stem and wrap it around the stamen.

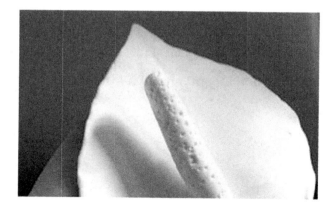

Wrap the petal around the stamen from one side (you can start from left or right) and then the other side overlapping each other. Press the bottom part of the petal to the stem lightly.

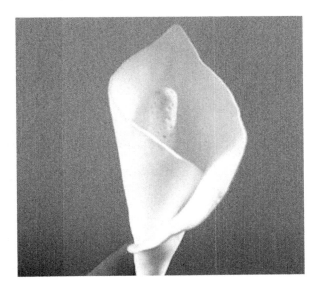

Clay Green Orchid Flower Made Easy

It's known as flower of energy, a symbol of nature, harmony and prosperity. Well, it would be a nice flower for birthday or wedding anniversary.

The best thing with green orchid clay is it will last for long, an everlasting bloom.

Let's have fun making this green orchid.

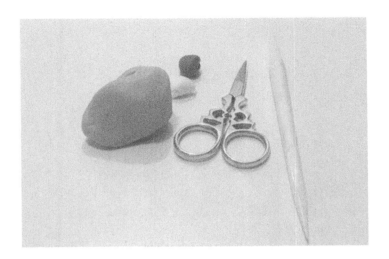

Steps to make clay green orchid flower:

First step is to make 5 equal clay ball shape

Slowly change the ball shape to a teardrop shape. Then, flatten the teardrop shape with your index finger and shape the side of the clay to make the petal.

Use your clay tool to make the vein. Don't panic If you don't have the tool. Use toothpick to draw the vein. Do it lightly.

Vary the direction of the petals and put it on top of your rolling pin or tissue to keep the petals stay in shape. Let them dry in room temperature.

Arrange those five petals on your table top (mine is kitchen bench) when it is about 75%. I want the petals to look natural so you'll see the 5 of them not exactly in the same size or shape.

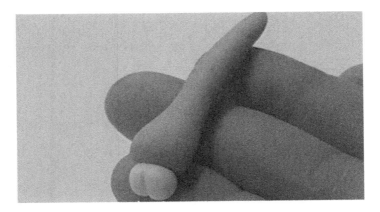

Next, make the column and lip. This would be the center of the flower.

Wrap the lip around the column like the picture below.

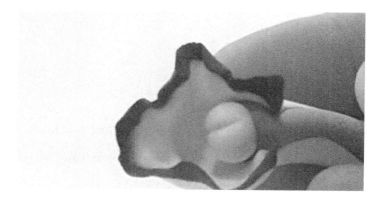

Finally, attach the petals one by one to the lip start with 2 petals in the left and right and then the 3 petals in between the two petals.

That's it. Enjoy your clay green orchid flower.

Below is finish flower from 2 angles. You can insert the stem if you want to make flower arrangement. Or, use it as brooch, pendant or earring for smaller green orchid.

Morning Glory Clay Flower Tutorial

Here you'll see our morning glory clay flower tutorial together with video to paint the clay after it's dry.

Steps to Make Morning Glory Clay

You need floral tape, wire for stem and stamen.

Bend the stamen to two part in unequal length, put it on top of the wire and wrap it with floral tape.

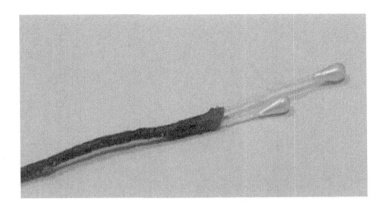

Take your homemade clay, knead well and roll it to the ball and then to teardrop clay basic shape.

Use your clay tool to hollow the teardrop shape.

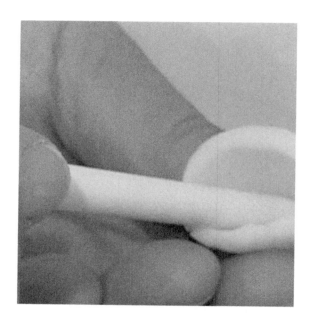

Spread the top part of the teardrop outward and flatten it like the picture beside.

The flower is ready now. Use kitchen towel to make a ring as a support and put the wet morning glory clay in the middle of tissue ring until it's dry.

This time, color your homemade clay with green acrylic paints color and make small teardrop shape from it.

Cut the green teardrop to two part and make teh shape like the picture beside.

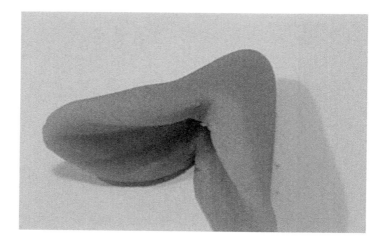

This green clay (calyx) will be attached at the bottom of the flower later on.

Next, insert the stamen that has been attached to the wire to the middle of the flower and add the calyx.

Leave the flower until it's dry completely in room temperature. After that, we can use acrylic paints to color the petal.

Poppy Flower Tutorial

Here you'll see poppy flower tutorial made of air dry clay.

I would think the clay version looks nice and appropriate for this event. We can make poppy clay for brooch or hat and hair accessories.

Red poppy symbolizes remembrance, worn during the day to remember those who served and died in war.

We hope this tutorial will contribute to everyone who is thinking to participate in the movement by making artificial poppy, in clay version this time.

Alright, let's check out our poppy flower tutorial.

Tools and materials:

We've used light-weight air dry clay as it is easy to handle and suitable for all ages. If you like, you can also use an oven-baked polymer clay.

Check our pros and cons between these two type of clay at "what clay to buy" page.

In fact, homemade clay would be good too.

Beside of clay, you'll need glue to paste the petals to the center of the flower. PVA glue or school glue is good enough for air dry clay.

As for the tool, you'll only need scissor. But, I also like to use clay scraper. This is one of my favorite clay tools.

Poppy Flower Tutorial guide:

Step 1:

We start with the center of the flower. We used clay scraper to cute the green clay to eight section and then use scissor to pull up the edges and pinch the corner to make it sharp. It looks like a star on the stump.

Step 2:

Honestly I don't know the name of this part but make something like giant eye lashes :)

Step 3:

Wrap around those you make in step 2 to the center of the flower.

Step 4:

Make 4 poppy petals, 2 pieces larger than the other 2.

You can start with ball shape, change it to teardrops, flatten it and use your clay tool to make the line marks on the petals.

We use toilet roll to make a backing for the petal so it will stay in shape until its dry.

Step 5:

Glue the petal one by one to the center of the flower. Our poppy clay is done now.

Gerbera Daisy Clay Ring Tutorial

Gerbera daisy clay ring for Mother's day gift? Why not? It's unique, fashionable and may not be sold in the stores.

I am sure mum who receive this humble clay ring will be happy, especially if it is hand-made by her loved ones.

Steps to make gerbera daisy clay ring:

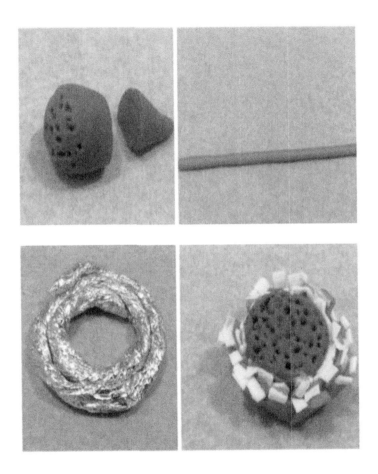

Firstly, let's make the center of the flower. Roll the clay (any color you like) to a ball shape and then change it to a tear drop shape.

Poke the top part with clay tool or toothpick and then cut the bottom part of the teardrop.

For stamen, roll small spaghetti shape clay or a rope - I use red color in the above picture. Add thin white rope and attach it to the red one.

Use rolling pin to press the two colors together.

Use scissor to cut the clay from the white part. I like the stamen to look natural so I don't really care about its uniformity.

After that, wrap the stamen around the center of the flower. Leave it in the room temperature and let it dry.

I used cold porcelain clay for this tutorial. Sometimes, it's not easy to get the clay to stand by itsel when its still soft and wet. So, I've made a prop with aluminium foil.

Flowers Clay

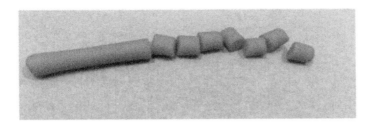

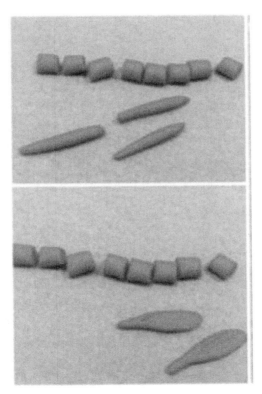

39

For petals, roll the clay to spaghetti shape and make about 20 to 25 pieces of short pieces.

Roll those small pieces to teardrop shapes, press it and add the veneer. I didn't use mold or ready-made cutter for the petal. Some perfectionist people may see my creation as messy and untidy. But, I like it this way. It looks more natural to me.

Arrange the petal on top of the aluminium foil ring. Add the glue to secure the petals and press the middle part with clay ball tool.

Finally paste the stamen to the center of the petals.

Leave it to dry.

Pansy Clay Tutorial

This pansy clay color may look a little bit funny to some of you

Well, I've intentionally made the pansy flower in dark purple color as a ring to match my friend's evening gown. Yes, I'll give this to my friend as a gift.

Steps to make pansy clay:

Let's make 5 teardrop clay shapes as a start.

Flatten the teardrop shape on your palm by pressing it with your index finger. Use your clay tool to make the vein and pull the side of the petal randomly.

Make 5 flower petals and arrange it by overlapping one to another. Add glue at the back of the petals.

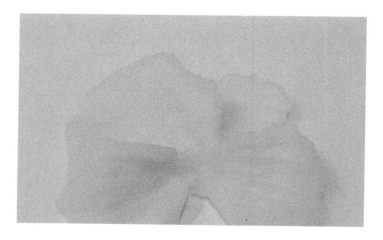

Here you can see that all five petals has been arranged nicely.

Leave the petals for 1 or 2 days until it's dry completely. I wanted to use this flower as a ring, so I paste the flower to the metal ring base with super glue.

By the way, I've used oil paints this time but I would think watercolor or acrylic paints (water base paints) is better for homemade clay.

Honestly, I am not really happy with my flower project this time. It seems that the clay was not performing as good as I expected.

Probably, it's better to stick with cold porcelain clay or homemade clay with flour base if you want to make clay flower.

Personally, I like soft clay for flower making. It's easy to handle, light and still a little bit flexible when it's dry even though it's not translucent like cold porcelain clay.

It's a good experience and experiment anyway. It's a good lesson to learn. I am sharing my experience with you so you will have a better result when making this pansy.

Alright! here is my version of pansy flower.

How To Make A Gum Paste Peony

Materials:

Gum paste (white or colored pink in your chosen color. You would also need a little green gum paste if you decide to make peony buds)

Rolling pin

Peony petal cutters:

Colette Peters

Sunflower Sugar Art

Special petal veiner:

Peony flower veiner

Round Styrofoam balls 1 1/2" or smaller for peony buds

#20 gauge wire

#24/26 gauge wire

Green floral tape

Craft glue

Chocolate egg mold

Apple foam trays (you can get those at your local grocery store)

Powdered food colors (Matching the color of the gum paste. Remember green color for buds)

Cornstarch

Brushes (for coloring the peony and for the tylo glue)

Ball tool

Foam pad

Small pieces of foam/paper

Square piece of thin flexible foam about 6"x6"

Large piece of styrofoam/cake dummy

Tall drinking glass

Plastic bag/zipper bag (stops the petals from drying, while you work)

Cel board

5 petal flower cutter (1" or a little bigger)

Peony cutters:

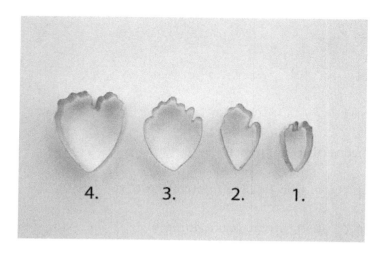

Step 1:

Cut three pieces of #20 gauge wire. It should be long enough so that you can bend the end, when you need to hang the peony, upside down while drying. You can always trim the length when you are finished with the flower. Wrap some green floral tape tight around the wires. Starting about 1/2" down. Next dip the end of the wires, in some craft glue and insert the wire into the 1 1/2" styrofoam ball. Make sure, that you don't push it all the way through the styro ball. You should be stopping where the floral tape starts.

Note: As you may have noticed. I do not have any floral tape on my wire. Somehow I was not able to find my floral tape, so that's why I have used a piece of gauge wire instead. I will replace the photo when I have found the lost floral wire.

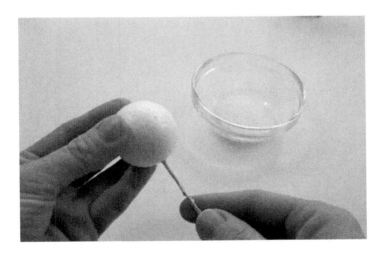

Step 2:

Knead the gum paste pliable and roll it out to about 1-2mm thickness. Take the smallest peony cutter (1) and cut out 8 petals.

Place them in the plastic bag as you cut them.

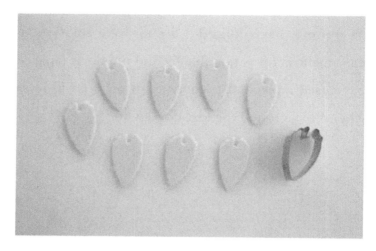

Step 3:

Take the "peony flower veiner". Lightly dust with a little cornstarch and place a petal at the bottom of the veiner. Remember to place the "front" of the petal down towards the veiner. Now rub your finger with a little cornstarch and gently push the petal into the veiner. Be careful not to push to hard or you may ruin the petal. Gently lift off the petal and turn it over. Your petal should now look, just like the petal on the photo. Place it back in the plastic bag and continue with the rest of the small petals.

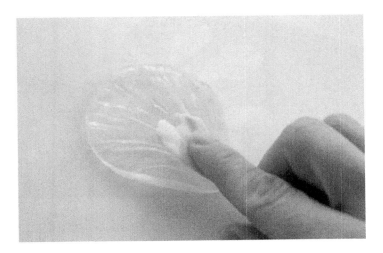

Step 4:

Take your foam pad and the ball tool. Place a petal, backside up and gently start to frill/thin the edge of the petal. Frill only the top half of the petal. Again place them in the plastic bag as you go.

Note: Decide for yourself how frilly you want the petals to be. Just be careful, not to tear the edge of the petal when you use the ball tool

Step 5:

Take the styro ball and 2 petals. Brush a little glue on the back of the petals and place the petals, so that they overlap the top of the ball.

Step 6:

Brush tylo glue on the rest of the petals and arrange the remaining 6 petals around the styro ball. Make sure that you do not cover the top of the peony. You should be able to see the first 2 petals. Set aside the styro ball in a large piece of styrofoam and move on to step 7.

Step 7:

Take the chocolate egg mold and lightly dust it with a little cornstarch. Then roll out more gum paste and take the next size peony cutter (2) and cut out 8-10 petals. Repeat steps 3 to 4, but instead of placing the petals in the plastic bag. Place the petals in the chocolate egg mold, backside up. Let them slightly dry for 20-30 minutes.

Tip! If you only have a mold for 8 eggs and need more molds. Then, make your own mold by pressing 5-10 sheets of foil over the egg shells. Voila! a quick and easy homemade mold.

Step 8:

When the petals have slightly dried. Brush a little glue on the back and arrange all the petals so they overlap around the styro ball. Take the peony and gently press it into your cupped hand, to shape the petals. They should slightly bend towards the center.

Note: On the photo, the petals have not been "cupped" with my hand.

Step 9:

Hang the peony upside down, on a safe place (away from cats and kids) and let it dry overnight.

Step 10:

This is how it looks when it have dried overnight.

Let's continue with the peony.

Step 1:

Roll out the gum paste and cut out 8 petals using the next peony petal cutter (3). Repeat the steps 3-4 from the peony tutorial part 1 for the petals and then place the petals in the chocolate egg mold, backside up. Let them dry for 20 mins.

Next brush a little tylo glue on the petal but only at the bottom of the petal. Arrange all the petals, so they overlap around the second layer of petals. Hang it upside down while you prepare for the next step.

Step 2:

Take a tall drinking glass and push the wire through the foam and let the peony rest in the glass. Then take small pieces of kitchen paper and carefully place them in between the petals, to give them a little shape. Allow to dry for at least 6 hours or more. I let my peony dry overnight.

Step 3:

When the petals are dry, remove the pieces of paper (save for later).
Place the peony in styrofoam/cake dummy while you are preparing
the last row of petals for the peony.

Printed in Great Britain
by Amazon

42772579R00040